# MODERNJAZZ
## STANDARDSFORGUITAR

Over 60 Original Modern Jazz Tunes by Artists Including: Mike Stern, John Scofield, Pat Martino, Gilad Hekselman, Bill Frisell, Kurt Rosenwinkel, Ozy Noy & Many More

Executive Editor
### JOELHARRISON

FUNDAMENTALCHANGES

# Modern Jazz Standards For Guitar

**Over 60 Original Modern Jazz Tunes by Artists Including: Mike Stern, John Scofield, Pat Martino, Gilad Hekselman, Bill Frisell, Kurt Rosenwinkel, Oz Noy & Many More**

ISBN: 978-1-78933-396-1

For over 350 Free Guitar Lessons with Videos Check Out

**www.fundamental-changes.com**

Join our active Facebook community:

**www.facebook.com/groups/fundamentalguitar**

Tag us for a share on Instagram: **FundamentalChanges**

Instagram: **FundamentalChanges**

With special thanks to Pete Sklaroff for his assistance with notation.

**www.petesklaroff.com**

Cover Image Copyright: Shutterstock, danymages

# Contents

# Foreword

## By Joel Harrison

There was a time when one could go to a jazz show and hear tunes that stayed mostly within a certain tradition. Artists like Wes Montgomery, Grant Green, and Herb Ellis penned their own compositions, but the writing fell within the parameters of swing, bebop, and the Great American Song Book.

Today's jazz composing, especially on guitar, has morphed into a vast, diverse array of sound-worlds, approaches and languages. Perhaps there is still a *lingua franca* beneath it all, but it is being taken apart and put back together in enough ways to make your head spin. Nearly every band leader writes their own music now, and good luck finding two people whose approach is the same on any given night.

Yet, when a jam session occurs, in all likelihood you'll hear the same tunes that people have been playing for decades; pieces by Monk, Miles, Ornette, Gershwin, etc. So, it eventually occurred to me, "Why aren't we playing each other's compositions? I've been listening to Nels Cline for 45 years and I've never played one of his charts!"

I began to get curious about what it might teach us all to play some of the contemporary classics penned by the pioneers of modern jazz guitar. I love the shared language of the past and the way it bonds us, but what about the language (or diverse languages) of today?

With this in mind, I contacted as many guitar-playing composers as I could, and the result is the book in your hands: a collection of modern standards that give insight into the melodic and harmonic thought of some of the greatest players on the planet. It's wonderful to see the variety, overwhelming even. And that, of course, is a hallmark of the Alternative Guitar Summit – the event I run that regularly brings together many of the contributors.

Some of the tunes here are conventional lead sheets – melody and chords. Others might cause you to ask, "What does this mean, and how the heck can I improvise on it?" I advise listening to the artist's recordings to capture the essence of each piece.

For rights reasons, we were not allowed to simply give you mp3s to download, but we tracked down the majority of the compositions on Spotify and put them together in a playlist. Open the Spotify app and scan the code below to get it:

Alternatively, go to this URL: **https://spoti.fi/3PkroGh** via your web browser.

A handful of the tunes were not available on Spotify but may be found on Apple Music or even YouTube.

Listen to the music, study the charts, then get together with a pal and wade in! If a song is too hard (and some of them *are* hard) start with an easy one and work your way forward. Luxuriate in all the ways your fellow players manage to use the same 12 notes.

Over decades of using the Real Book, I've noticed that there are a few dozen songs that everyone plays, while countless others are wonderful side dishes. I wonder which pieces in this compilation will find wider popularity and which will remain niche but important harmonic studies? The point is this: *consciousness loves contrast*. Seeing the infinite ways that modern-day guitarists shape their material will inevitably inspire you in shaping your own, and if you write your own material, there is much to learn here.

Lastly, when putting together a compilation such as this, one undertakes an impossible task and some important names have inevitably been left out. Some artists had existing publishing agreements they could not violate. Others were too busy pursuing current projects to contribute. Still others may have inadvertently been left out by me! But consider this book to be a vast, yet incomplete, snapshot of the protean landscape. It's an important volume that documents the scope, color and creativity of modern jazz guitar. I hope you enjoy exploring it!

*Joel Harrison*

*Executive Editor*

*New York City*

# About the Editor

Guitarist, composer, arranger, lyricist, writer, educator, and vocalist Joel Harrison has "created a new blueprint for jazz" (New Orleans Times-Picayune). He is a Guggenheim Fellow (2010) whose compositions have been commissioned by Chamber Music America, Meet the Composer, New Music USA, the Jerome Foundation, NYSCA, and the Mary Flagler Cary Trust. He has released 23 CDs as a leader on seven different labels. Harrison's music may be founded on jazz but veers into classical, rock, country, and all manner of American roots music. Succinctly described by the New York Times as "protean… brilliant" he is also an active film composer, having worked on the Oscar-nominated *Traffic Stop* and the Sundance awardee *Southern Comfort*.

Harrison is the founder and director of the Alternative Guitar Summit, a yearly festival devoted to new and unusual guitar music. Pat Metheny has called the Summit "one of the most interesting and distinguished forums for guitar on the planet."

Harrison is also the author of *Guitar Talk: Conversations with Visionary Players*.

**https://bit.ly/3PEjrvn**

**www.joelharrison.com**

## The Alternative Guitar Summit

Founded in 2010 by guitarist/composer Joel Harrison, this is a yearly concert series and summer camp of daring, inventive players who emphasize new and unusual approaches to the guitar. The music we present celebrates the guitar's enormous range, beyond style or genre.

The AGS seeks to commission new work, whether improvised, notated, or both, and is devoted to promoting new music through education and performance. We aspire to provide opportunities for lesser known, non-commercial musicians.

**www.alternativeguitarsummit.com**

# 11th Hour Blues
**David Gilmore**

# Absalom

**Adam Rogers**

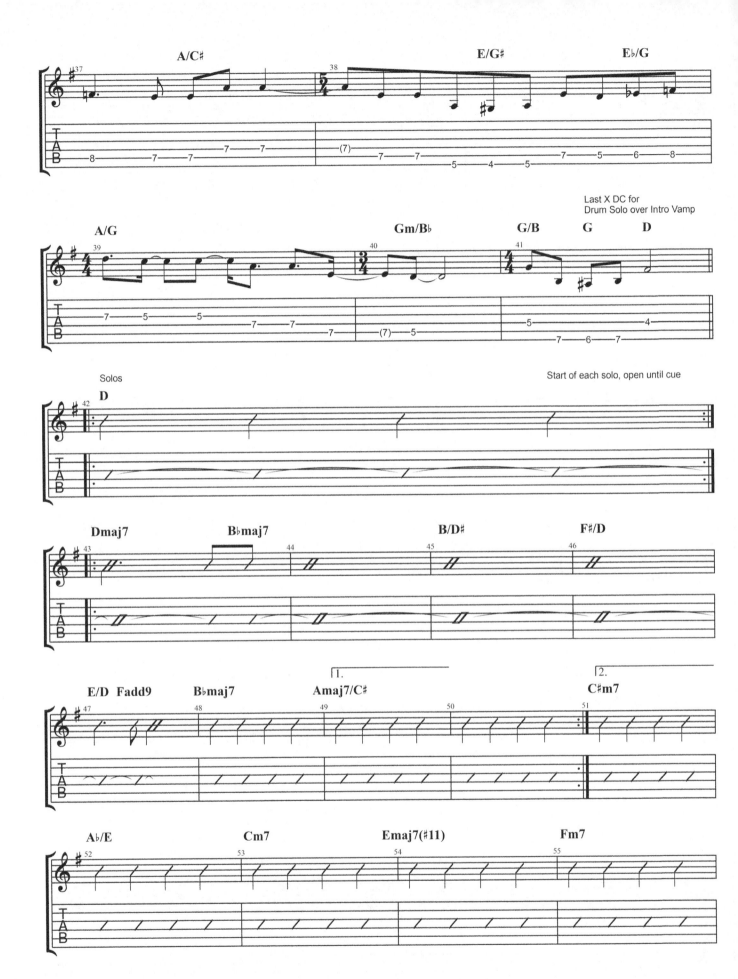

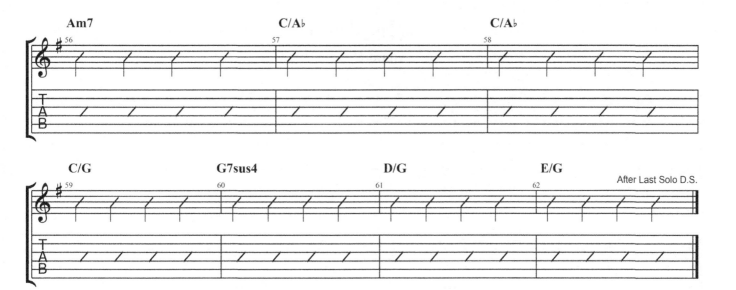

# Absalom

**Adam Rogers**

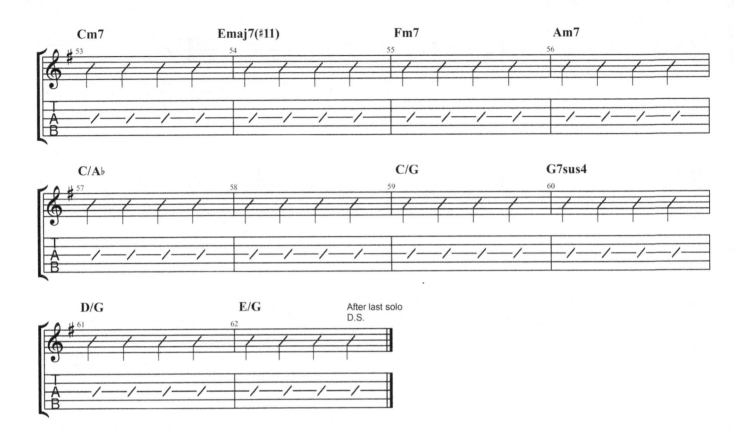

# Actual Ballad
## (The Memory of Jazz)
### John Schott

# Aestivation

**Liberty Ellman**

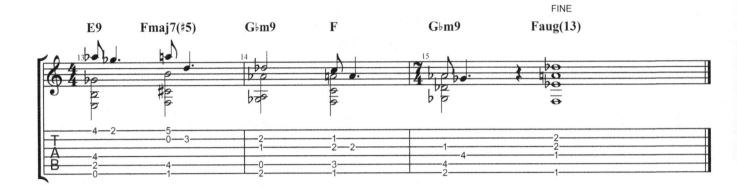

# A Few Dozen

**Bruce Arnold**

# A Few Dozen

**Bruce Arnold**

# Anthem For A New World

**Brandon Ross**

# Anthem For A New World
## Brandon Ross

# Balata
**Steve Cardenas**

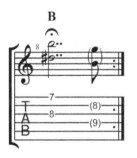

# Berry Drive

**John Pisano**

# Breathless

## Gilad Hekselman

# Calisthenics
## Cecil Alexander

# Calisthenics
## Cecil Alexander

# Chandelle

**Elliot Sharp**

improvisation......

# Chandelle
## Elliot Sharp

# Chocolate Souffle

## Oz Noy

# Chromazone
**Mike Stern**

42

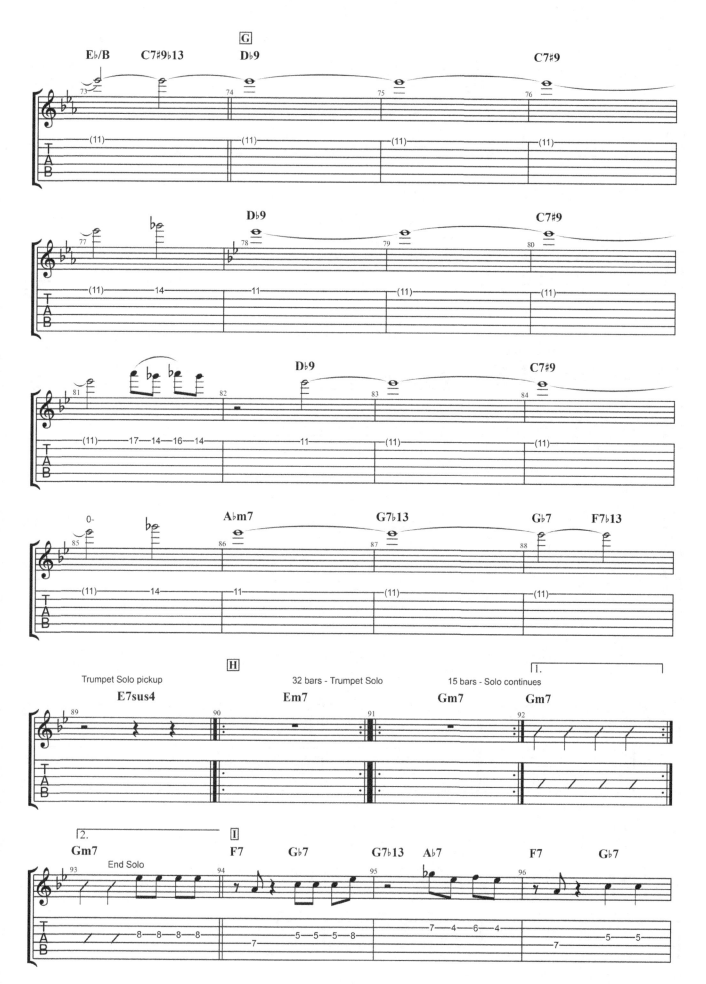

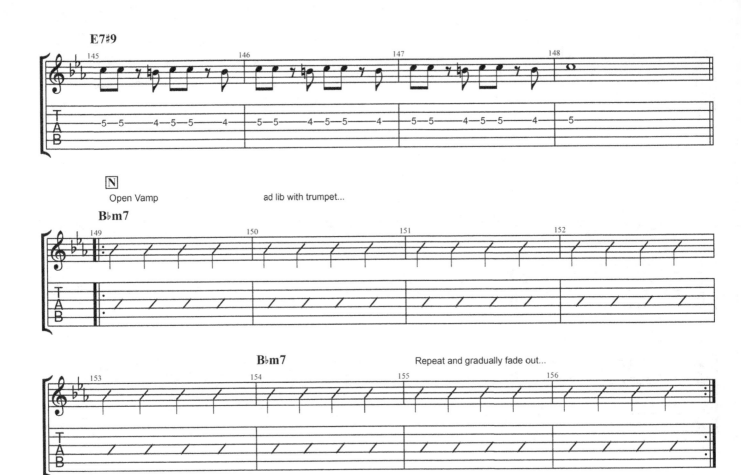

# Chromazone
## Mike Stern

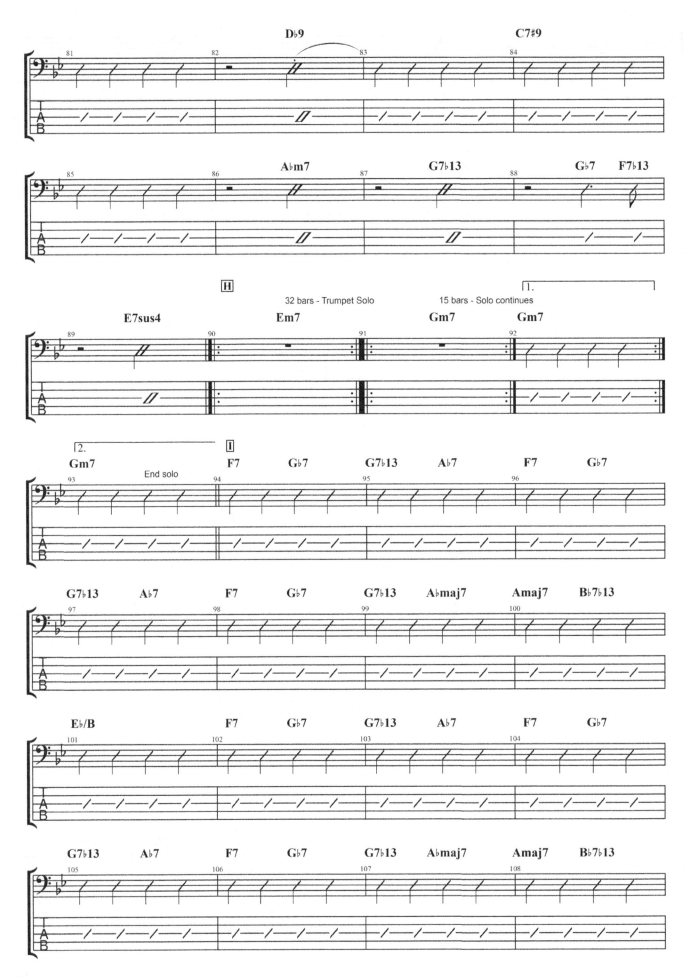

# Co-op Shift
**Amanda Monaco**

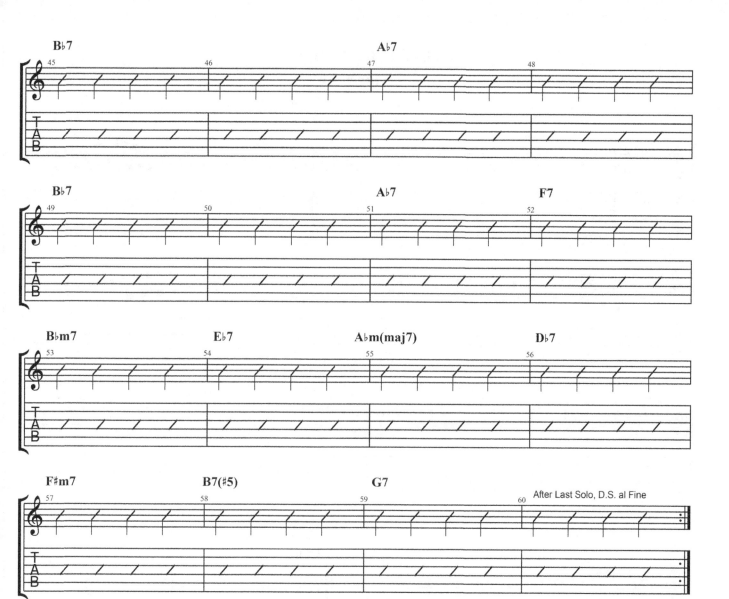

# Coromandel

### Nguyên Lê

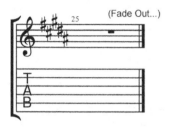

# Coronation
## Nir Felder

End on Cmaj7sus4/E

# Country Road
**Pat Martino**

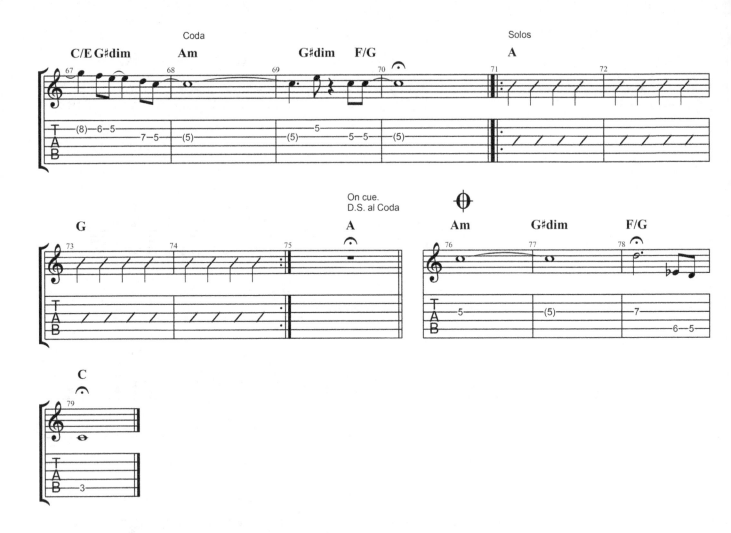

# Dream
## Nir Felder

# Dream
### Nir Felder

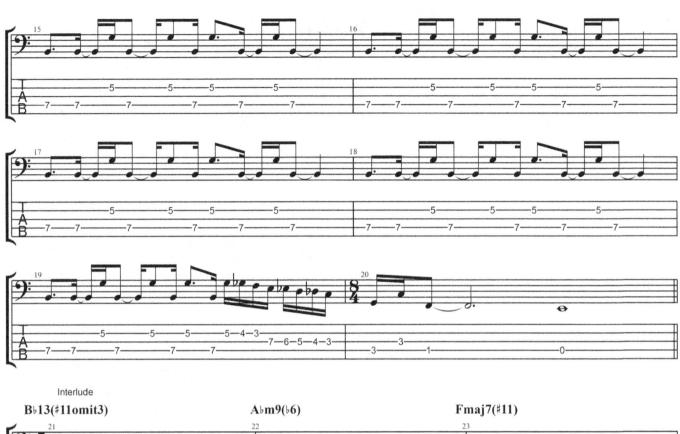

Interlude

B♭13(♯11omit3)          A♭m9(♭6)          Fmaj7(♯11)

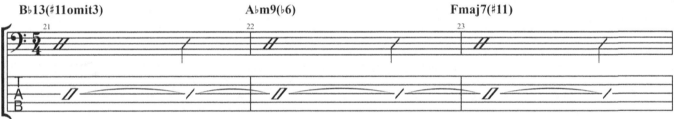

Form: 4 bars guitar upfront / 8 bars band in.

A section / 4 bars groove
A section / B section
A section / Interlude
Solos on A section to blues form / cue 4 bars groove, then B
A out and Fine

F♯7sus4          Fmaj7(♯11)          Fmaj7(♯11)

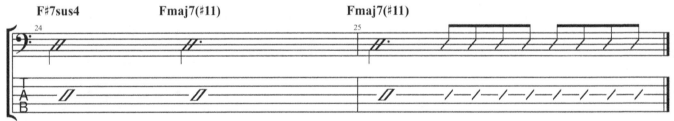

# Episode
## Brad Shepik

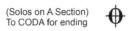

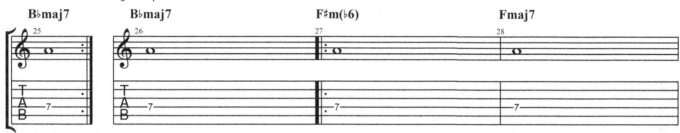

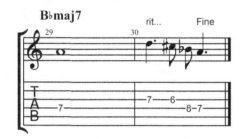

# Five Senses

### Nguyên Lê

# Freakadelic

**Jeff Parker**

# Gone

**Mike Stern**

# Gone
**Mike Stern**

# Hall

**Brad Shepik**

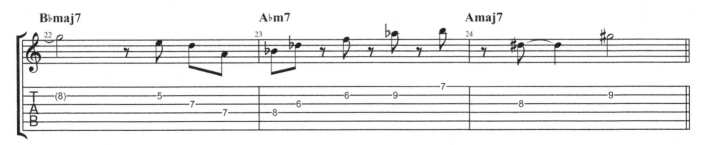

(Play 8 Bars on D7sus)

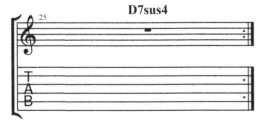

# Hangover
## John Scofield

Form: AAB
End: Play B Twice
End on Bbmin7

# Holy Butter

**Rez Abbasi**

88

# How Many Miles?

**Bill Frisell**

# I Can Remember

## Pete McCann

# In Due Course

**Kenny Wessel**

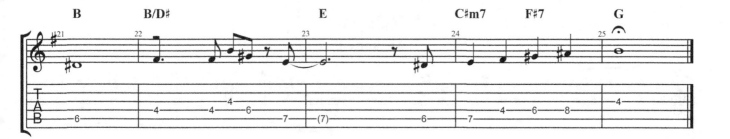

95

# Interlude 1

**Anthony Pirog**

# Ira (a split decision)
## Cecil Alexander

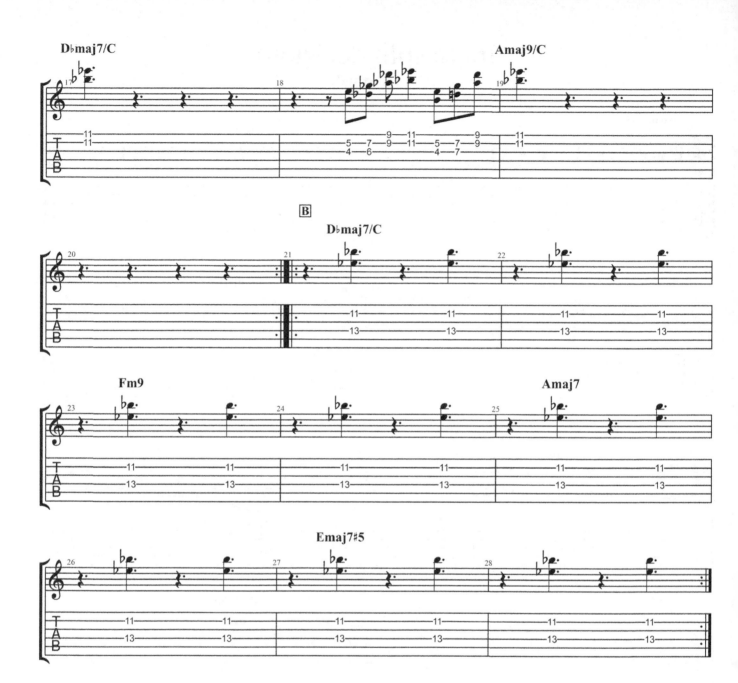

# Ira (a split decision)
## Cecil Alexander

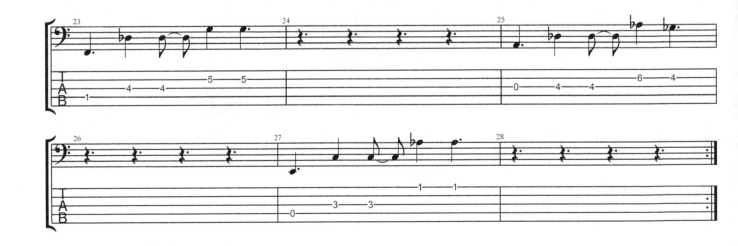

# It Will Get Better

### Gilad Hekselman

# Kudzu

## Miles Okazaki

# Kudzu

## Miles Okazaki

# Madhuvanti
**Anupam Shobhakar**

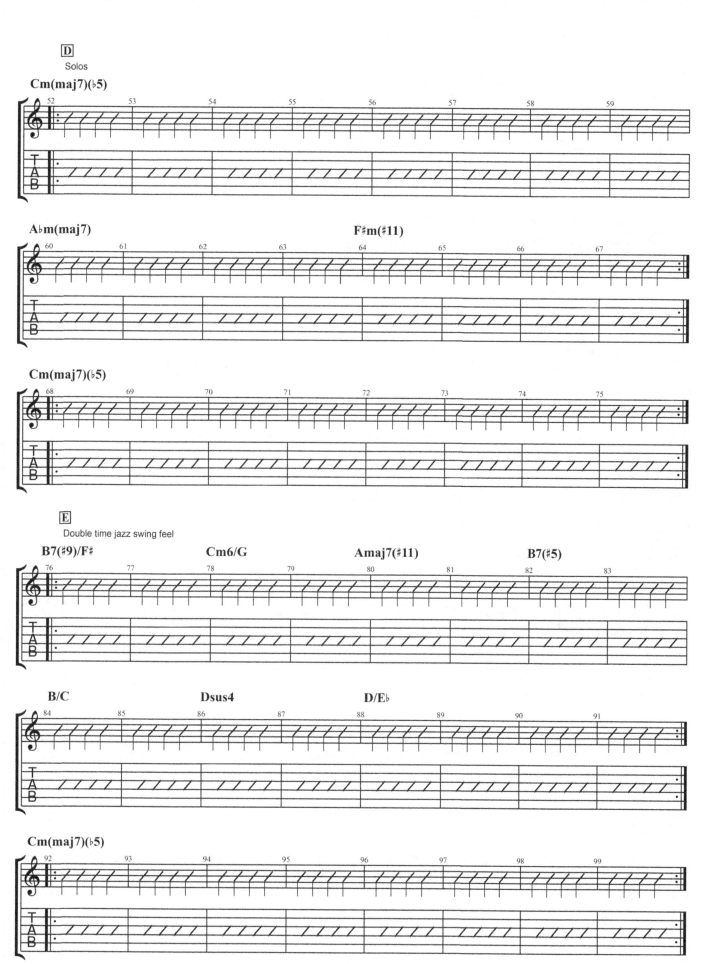

# MiCroy Tyner

**David Fiuczynski**

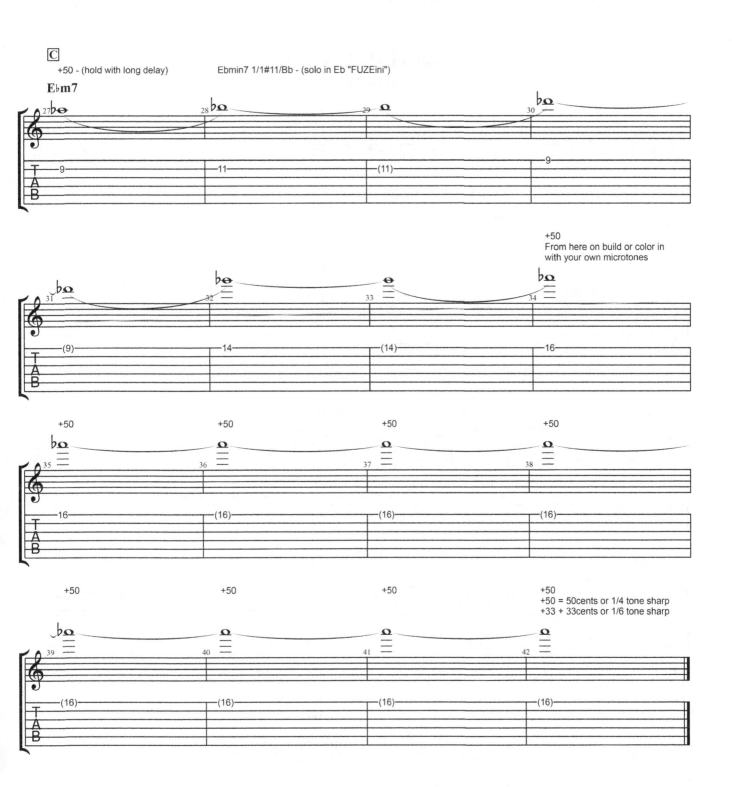

# Midnite Swim
## Sheryl Bailey

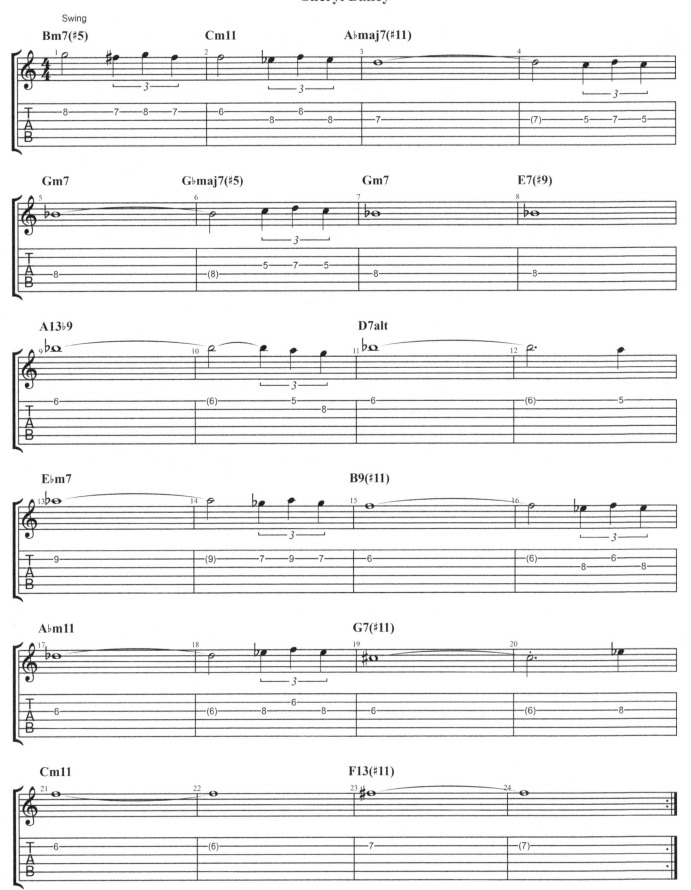

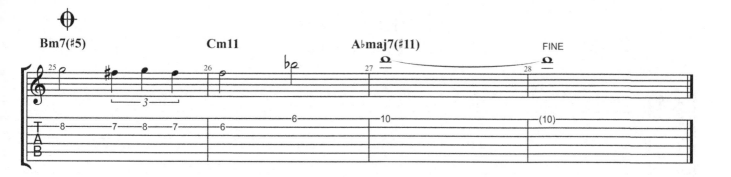

# Minor Blues

**Kurt Rosenwinkel**

Bass Figure

# Mitchum

**Adam Levy**

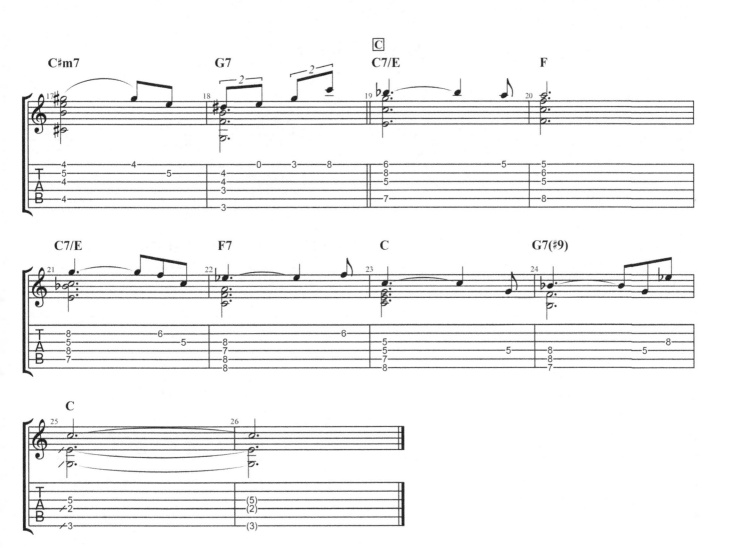

# New Moon
## Steve Cardenas

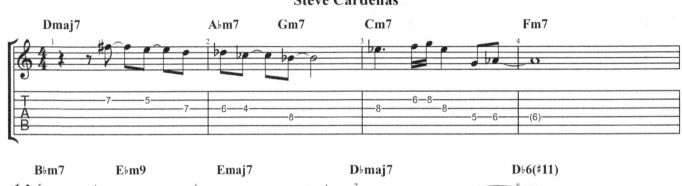

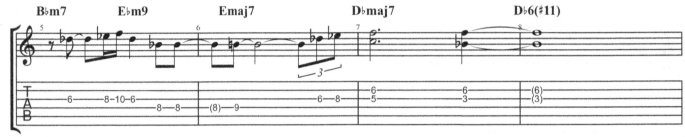

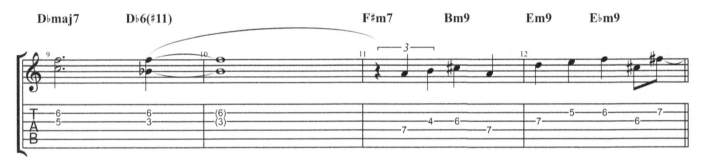

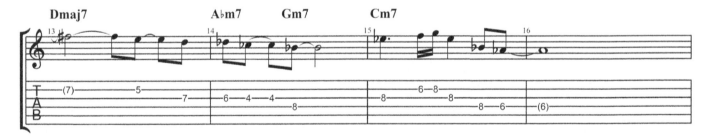

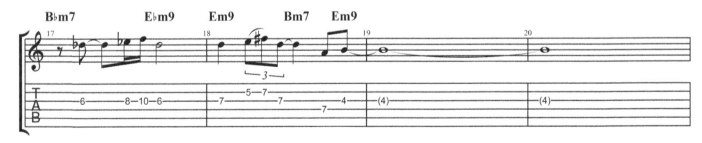

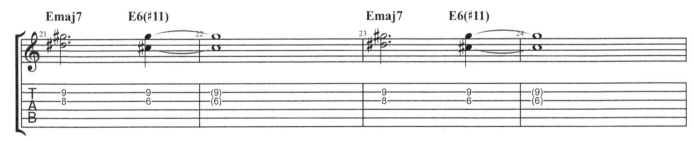

# Not Too Fancy

**Will Bernard**

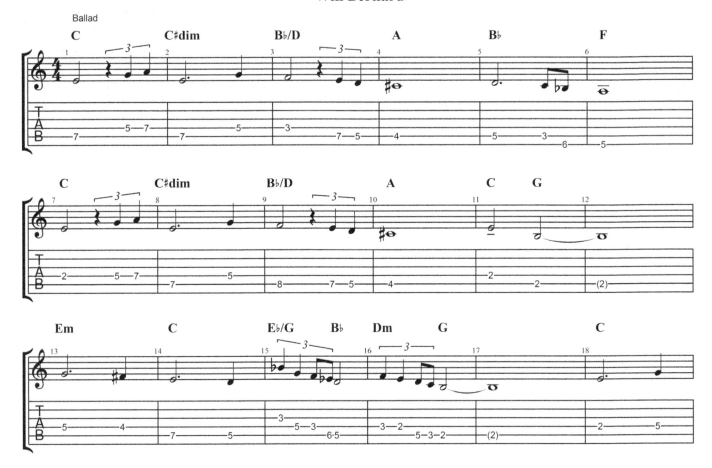

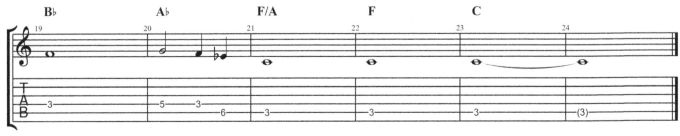

# Of Two Minds

**Kenny Wessel**

# Pocket Poem

**Anthony Pirog**

# Procession

**Anders Nilsson**

Tune low E string to F
Let ring if poss..

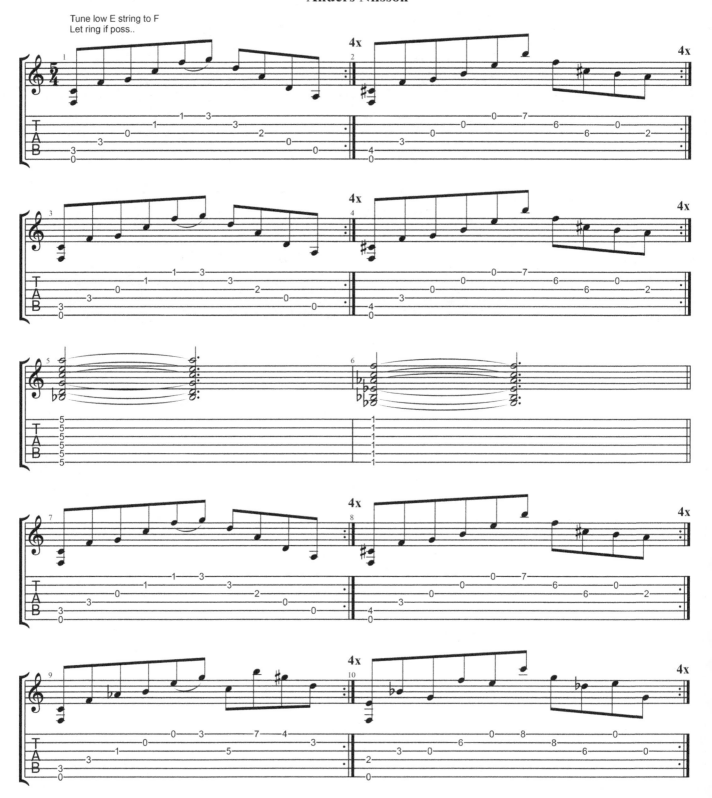

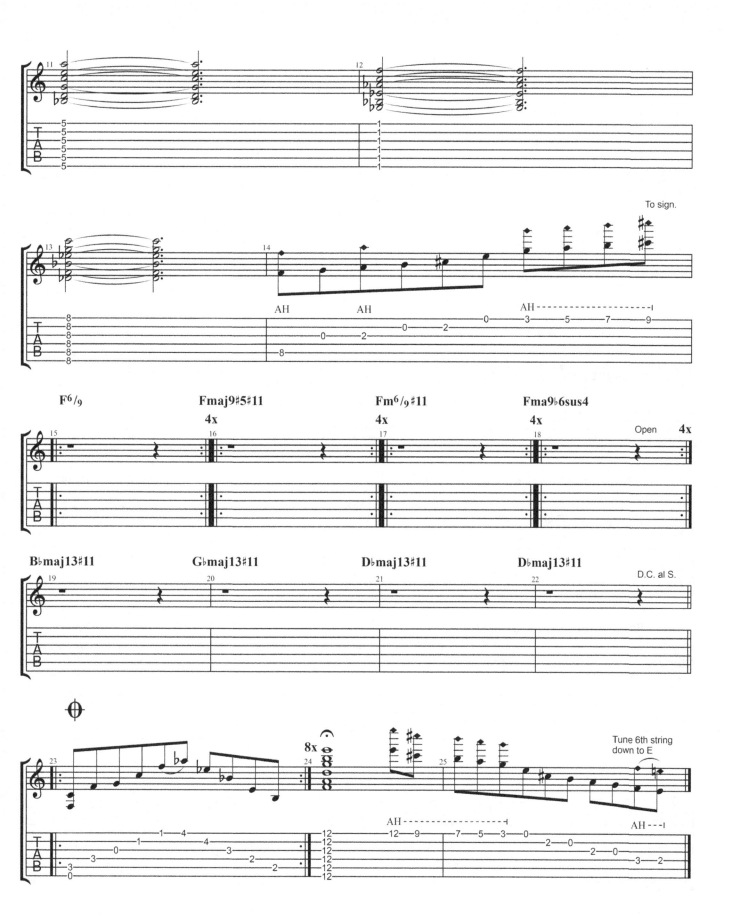

# Sacred Pause

**David Gilmore**

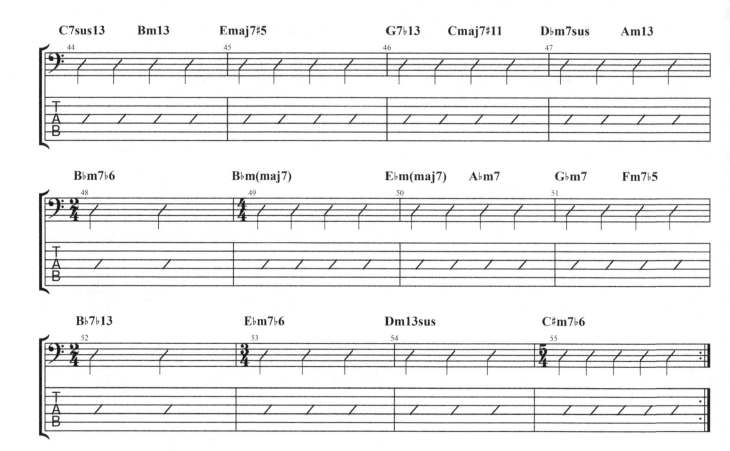

# Sacred Pause

**David Gilmore**

Continue with bass part on guitar part

# Seeing You

## Gilad Hekselman

# Seeing You

## Gilad Hekselman

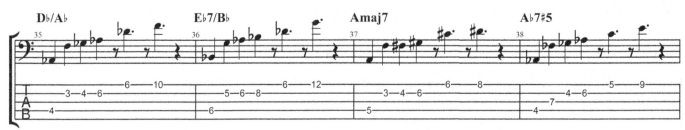

# Selfconscious-Lee

**John Schott**

136

# Starbrite

**Sheryl Bailey**

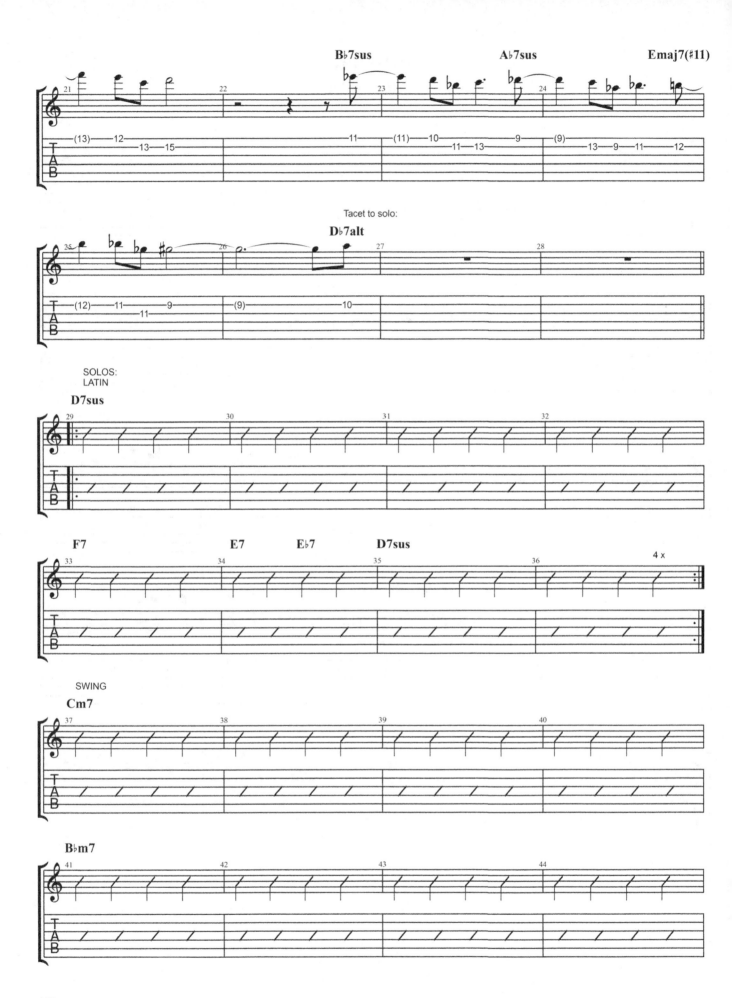

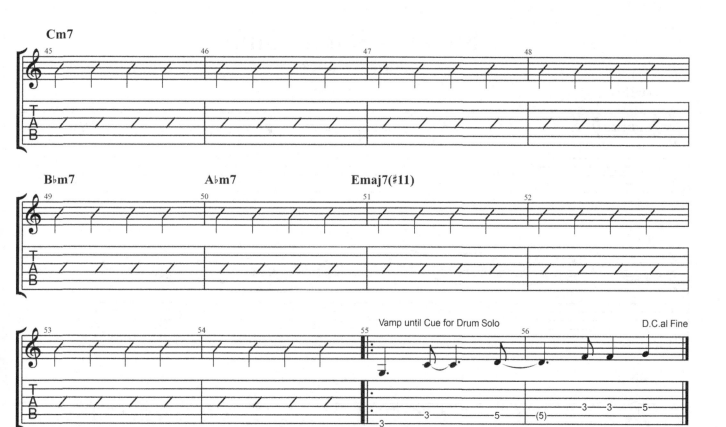

# Summer Band Camp

**Mick Goodrick**

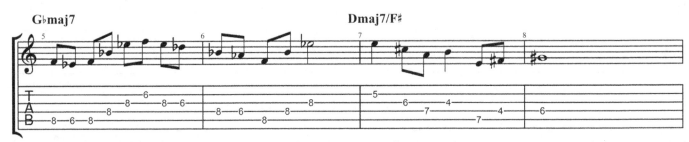

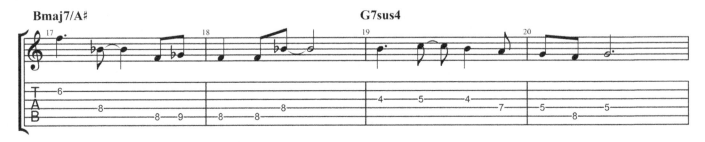

# Sunday Night With Vic

### Joel Harrison

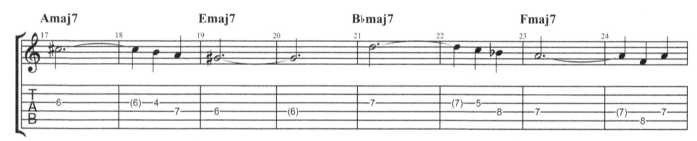

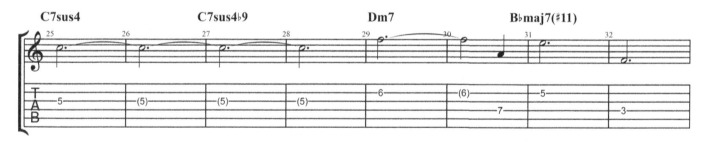

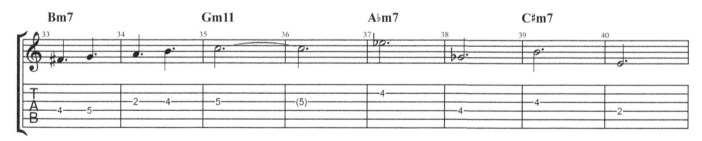

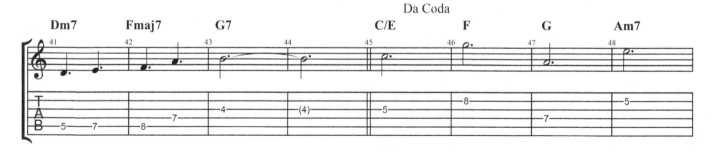

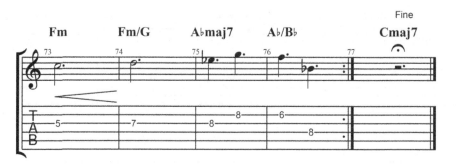

# Thankful
**Bill Frisell**

# That Old Sound (No. 27)

**Mary Halvorson**

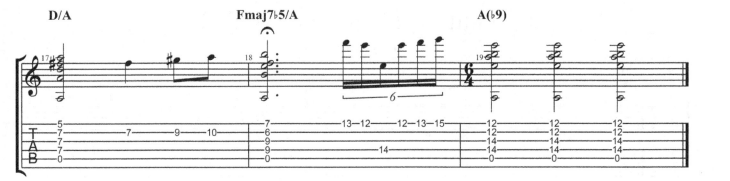

# That Old Sound (No. 27)
## Mary Halvorson

# The Bed We Made

### Nels Cline

150

# The Cat Stole The Moon
## Leni Stern

Solo over D or A pedal and end with opening lick.

# The Great Flood
## Bill Frisell

# The Great Flood
## Bill Frisell

# The Henrysons

## Wolfgang Muthspiel

Legatissimo and round
Electric Guitar

play like a shadow of guitar II

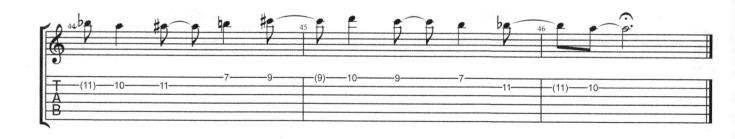

# The Henrysons

## Wolfgang Muthspiel

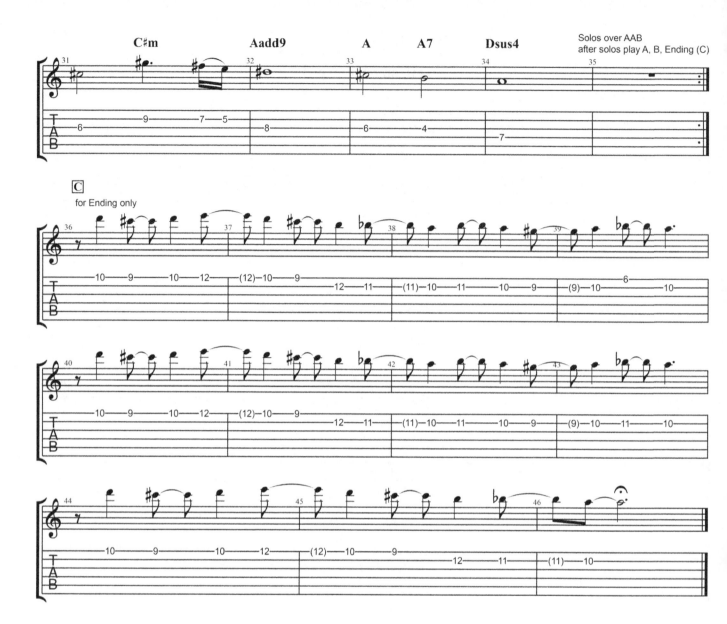

# The Henrysons

## Wolfgang Muthspiel

Solos over AAB
after solos play A, B, Ending (C)

162

# The Sip
## Liberty Ellman

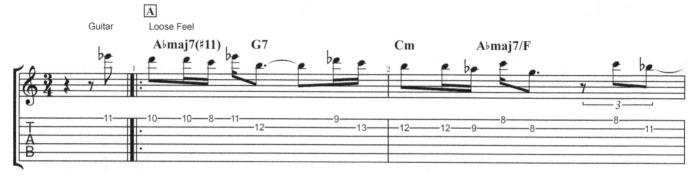

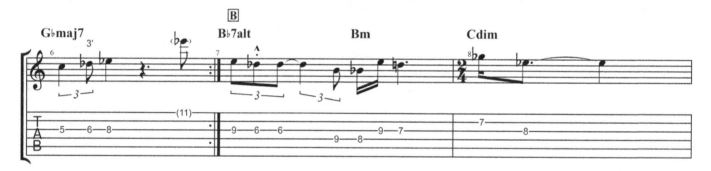

Form: AAB. AABB on Head Out

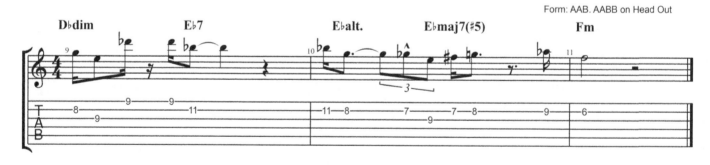

# The Sip
## Liberty Ellman

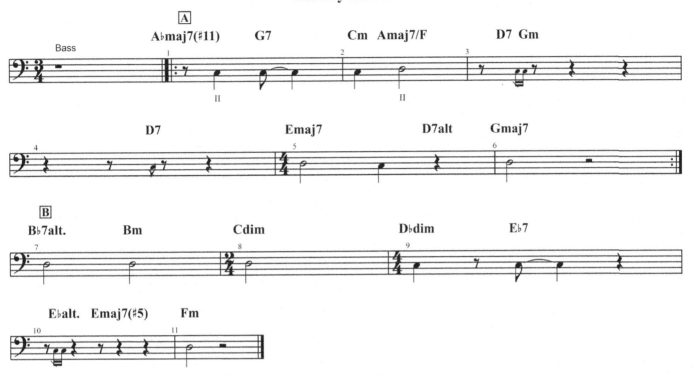

# There's Never Enough Time

**Joel Harrison**

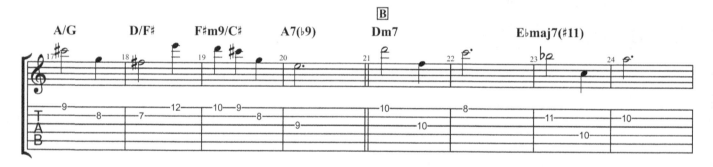

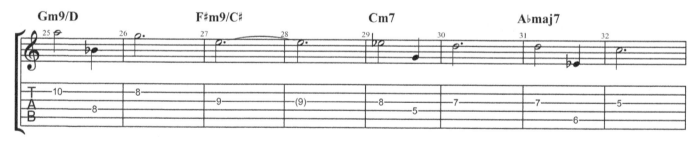

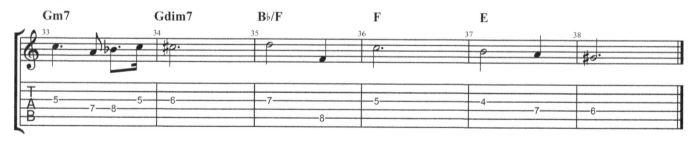

# Up On The Hill (for Andrew Hill)

**Rez Abbasi**

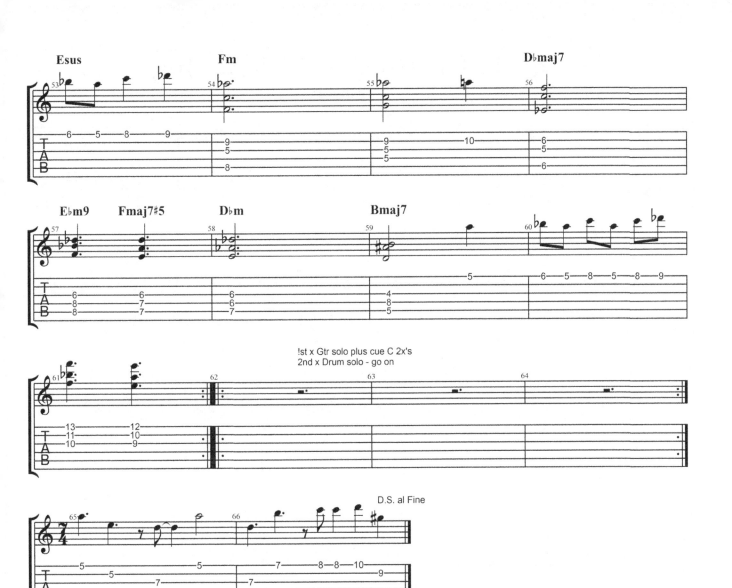

# Up On The Hill (for Andrew Hill)

**Rez Abbasi**

D.S. al Fine

# Uptown
## Wolfgang Muthspiel

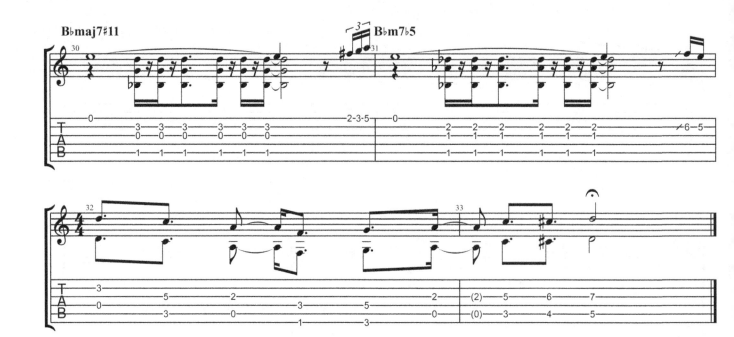

# Uptown
## Wolfgang Muthspiel

# Use of Light

**Kurt Rosenwinkel**

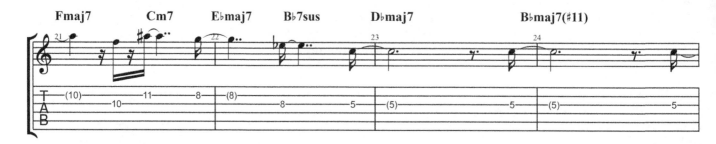

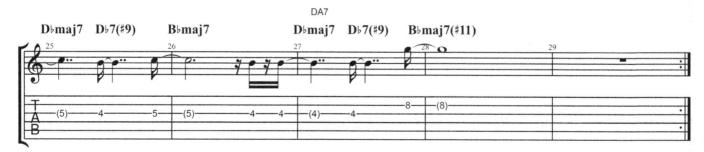

# Very Tall

**Adam Levy**

181

# Wheel

**Miles Okazaki**

Feel 8th note as 1/4 note,
move towards improvisation,
additional canon melody:

# Ying Hua (Sakura)

**David Fiuczynski**

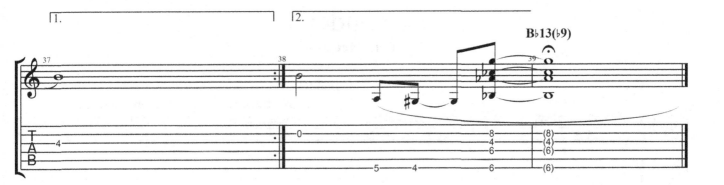

# Yonder
## Pete McCann

Solo over A B and C.
Head out take Coda

To Coda

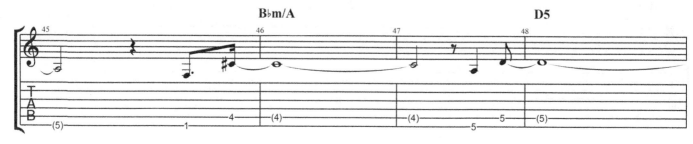

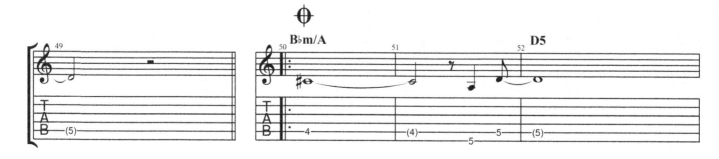

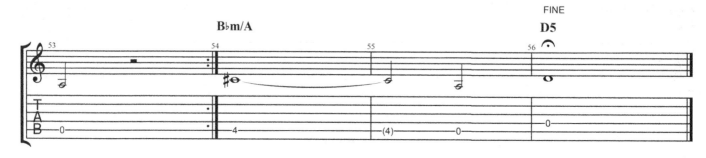

# You Were Meant For Me

**John Pisano**

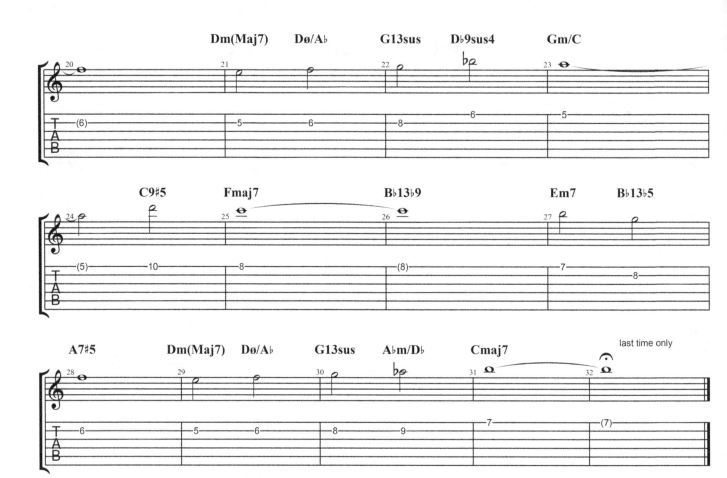

Made in the USA
Las Vegas, NV
25 September 2023